Whodini

Keith Elliot Greenberg

Lerner Publications Company
Minneapolis

Acknowledgements
The material in this book is based on an interview the author
conducted with members of Run-D.M.C., books and articles by
Steven Hager, Robert McCrum, William Cran, Robert MacNeil,
Charles E. Rogers, Steven Dougherty, E. Dottie Watkins, Toria J.
Smith, Barry Walters, John Piccarella, Robert Palmer, Pam Lambert,
John Milward, Jack Curry, Stephen Holden, Ed Kiersh,
Peter Blauner, and other sources.

Excerpt from "Hepster's Dictionary" by Cab Calloway,
published 1938, appears on p. 12.

LIBRARY OF CONGRESS CATALOGING-IN-PUBLICATION DATA

Greenberg, Keith Elliot.
    Rap/Keith Elliot Greenberg
        p.   cm.
    Summary: Discusses today's popular phenomenon of rap (a vocalist
tells a story to a rhythm background) and introduces some of the
most prominent rappers.
    ISBN 0-8225-1617-9 (lib. bdg.)
    1. Rapping (Music) — History and criticism — Juvenile literature.
2. Popular music — History and criticism — Juvenile literature.
3. United States — Popular culture — Juvenile literature.
[1. Rapping (Music) — History and criticism. 2. United States —
Popular culture.]   I. Title.
ML3477.G74   1987
784.5 — dc 19
                                                87-23264
                                                CIP
                                                AC MN

1   2   3   4   5   6   7   8   9   10   97   96   95   94   93   92   91   90   89   88

Contents

What is Rap? 7

Rap's Roots 11

Rap Vocabulary 17

Kings of Rock — Run-D.M.C. 21

Other Rappers 27

The Future of Rap 37

Run-D.M.C.

What Is Rap?

The beat has them bopping and the words have them thinking, from the tenement-lined streets of Harlem, New York, to the mansion parties of Beverly Hills, California. Rap music, once only popular with blacks in New York City, Washington, D.C., and Philadelphia, has grown to become America's freshest form of music, giving off energy found nowhere else. It seems that there's a new rap hit out every week, boasting, lecturing, and wisecracking.

While the vocalist or vocalists tell a story, the disc jockey provides the rhythm, operating the drum machine and "scratching"—rapidly moving the record back and forth under the needle to create rap's famous swishing sound. The beat can be traditional funk or heavy metal—anything goes. The most important part of rap is "rapping." Fans want to hear the lyrics.

7

During every generation, some old-fashioned, ill-humored people have become frightened by the sight of kids having a good time and have attacked the source of their pleasure. In the 1950s, the target was rock 'n' roll. Some claimed that the new type of music encouraged wild behavior and evil thoughts. Today, rap faces the same charges.

Those who condemn this exciting entertainment have never closely examined it. If they had, they would have discovered that rap permits kids to appreciate the English language by producing comical and meaningful poems set to music.

Rappers don't just walk on stage and talk off the top of their heads. They write their songs, and they put a lot of thought into them. Part of rapping is quick wit—rappers like L.L. Cool J and Run-D.M.C. grew up rapping in the neighborhood, and they learned to throw down a quick rhyme when they were challenged. But part of it is thoughtful work over many hours, getting the words to sound just right so that the ideas come across with style. As L.L. Cool J describes it, "I write all my songs down by hand. Each song starts with a word, like any other sentence, and becomes a manuscript."

Many performers set a positive example for their followers. Kurtis Blow rapped in a video for the March of Dimes' fundraising drive to battle birth defects and he has campaigned against teenage drinking as a spokesperson for the National Council on Alcoholism. On the television show "Reading Rainbow," Run-D.M.C. told viewers how books enabled them to become "kings of rock." On another occasion, group member Darryl "D.M.C." McDaniels said, "Little kids like to follow me around the neighborhood. I tell them to stay in school. Then I give them money to get something in the deli."

Run-D.M.C. is one of the numerous rap combos advising kids to keep off drugs. Doug E. Fresh and Grandmaster Flash have each made records telling of the horrors of cocaine. On Grandmaster Flash's hit "White Lines," he details how the drug can ruin a life, and shouts, "Don't do it!"

Says Run-D.M.C.'s Joseph "Run" Simmons, "Kids want to be like me, and if you want to be like me, you're good to go [a rap term meaning "in great shape"] because I don't stand for nothing bad."

Melle Mel

Rap's Roots

Although there are now rappers of all races, the music is the latest example of black pride in turning a phrase. The custom can be traced to Africa, where tribesmen hold "men of words" in high regard. In the same way that rap singers are admired for their rhymes, tribal leaders are madly applauded for their craftily-worded wisdom. Sometimes, delighted followers burst out in song upon hearing an exceptional message.

When black slaves were brought to the New World, members of a tribe were isolated from one another by ship captains who were fearful that slaves who talked to each other could plan a mutiny. Slaves using different dialects were forced to create a common language in order to communicate. This "pidgin English" or "creole" influenced the speech of whites living on the plantation. It eventually found its way into every corner of American society. Some words which can be directly linked to Africa are *banjo*, *banana*, *tote*, and *voodoo*.

On the plantation, blacks also mixed American music forms with beats they remembered from Africa. Like persecuted people everywhere, they found song to be a natural way of speaking out. It was also safer than revolution.

After the Civil War, blacks played a large part in composing jazz music. Jazz was similar to rap in that it had its own vocabulary. For instance, a male well-liked on the jazz scene was a "hepcat"—the 1930s version of a "b-boy." Just as the Fat Boys and Whodini would later write songs bragging about their rap skills, Cab Calloway crooned about his mastery of jazz lingo:

> *What's a hepcat? A hepcat is a guy*
> *Who knows all the answers, and I'm telling*
> *   you why . . .*
> *He's a high-falutin' student*
> *Of the Calloway vocab.*

Blacks also had a huge effect on rock 'n' roll, fashioning rhythm and blues in the 1950s and soul music in the 1960s. In the 1970s, rap developed in eastern cities out of this tradition of "black" music.

The grandfather of rap may be Clive Campbell, a Jamaica-born disc jockey known as "Herc" because of his muscular arms. In 1975, he was working at the Hevalo, a disco in a rundown section of the Bronx, New York. Herc was locally famous because he played rare

12

records like James Brown's "Give It Up or Turn It Loose" and the Jamaican-produced "Apache." But his specialty was that he didn't play full songs, just the most frantic sections—called "breaks"—over and over. The folks who danced acrobatically to Herc's break mixtures became known as "break dancers."

There's another story about the origin of the term "break dancing." Another young man in the Bronx had taught himself about African history and was determined not to let poverty defeat him. Afrika Bambaataa was a

Afrika Bambaataa (front) with his crew

respected disc jockey and the leader of the Zulu Kings, a gang that preferred music and dance to fighting. When the Zulu Kings were challenged by a local gang, Bambaataa suggested they take a break from the usual fighting and compete by dancing instead.

Bambaataa's music presentations were renowned for surprising or "bugging out" attendees. He often mixed funky dance tunes with the themes from television shows like "The Munsters" and "The Andy Griffith Show," amusing his audiences but still getting them onto the dance floor.

A competing disc jockey, "Grand Wizard" Theodore Livingston, changed music forever when he invented "scratching" while practicing at home. His technique was quickly copied all over the Bronx and in parts of neighboring Manhattan, New York.

But the gimmick that really launched rap was Joseph "Grandmaster Flash" Saddler's addition of emcees to his shows to talk to the audience over the music and keep them dancing. By 1978, these "rappers" were kings of the Bronx ballrooms.

In 1979, Sylvia Robinson, who had recorded hits like "Pillow Talk" and "Love Is Strange," walked into a New Jersey pizza shop and heard another customer playing a cassette tape of a Bronx rap show. Struck by the new, dynamic sound, she organized a group of rappers to record "Rappers' Delight" on the Sugarhill Records label. The tune sold an astounding two million copies!

14

As the music form spread around the country, New York groups like the Funky Four, Spoonie Gee, and the Treacherous Three picked up far-off followers. Run-D.M.C., a Queens, New York, trio, attracted white fans by using heavy metal and rock beats and writing lyrics that reflected their middle-class upbringing. In 1984, Run-D.M.C.'s self-titled debut album made history by "going gold"—selling 500,000 copies. The 1985 movie, *Krush Groove*, starring Run-D.M.C. and other rappers, introduced the music to millions more.

Perhaps rap's greatest monument is Run-D.M.C.'s video for "Walk This Way." It begins with the song's original performers, Steve Tyler and Joe Perry of the heavy metal band Aerosmith, on one side of a recording studio wall, and Run-D.M.C. on the other. At first, each group is angered by the other's noise. But finally the wall is broken and everyone sings together. The video not only symbolizes the joining of music styles, but the joining of races.

The Fat Boys

Rap Vocabulary

Just as jazz had its hepcats and rock 'n' roll had its cool players, rap has its b-boys. The new style of music comes with a new way of saying what you mean. This new vocabulary shows up in interviews with rappers, stories about rappers, and rap songs. Anyone who is interested in rap will bump into some of the words and phrases defined below. Of course, the language changes all of the time—soon these expressions will either sound as out of date as "hepcat" or as natural as "cool." Learn them while they're still hot.

b-boy: a popular, male rap music fan or performer

backspin: a disc jockey's way of maneuvering records on the turntable, usually repeating important beats or phrases

blaster: portable tape player

book out: leave

box: *See* blaster

break out: *See* book out

Tony Tone of the Cold Crush Brothers shows how to scratch as D.M.C. and Jam Master Jay look on. The rappers performed at a rally in support of the fight against apartheid in South Africa.

bug: weird

bug out: to confuse or impress

burn: to outshine a competitor

chill out or **chill:** relax

crew: a group of friends or partners

crush: beautiful female, as in, "She's crush;" to outshine or "burn" a competitor

cut: portion of a song played over and over

18

def: satisfactory or superior, as in, "That's a def set of speakers"

dis: disrespect; to express disrespect or to criticize

down: involved with

down by law: associated with something good; to have high status

fly: well-dressed; good-looking; satisfactory or superior

fresh: original

good to go: in great shape

hard: uncaring

hip-hop: rappable music; the lifestyle that includes rapping and break dancing

homeboy: friend from the neighborhood. *Also* **homey**

joint: the best, as in, "It's the joint!"

juice: power; money

kicks: shoes

MC: rap performer

mellow: close friend

scratch: move the record back and forth under the needle

shock the house: dazzle a party with something new, like an original disc jockey technique

snapping: to insult someone, usually in a joking way, as in, "Stop snapping on me, homeboy."

throw-down: a party; a fight; to throw down is to challenge someone

wack: stupid, as in, "Crack is wack"

word: "That's right." Said in agreement to a statement.

Run-D.M.C.

Kings of Rock— Run-D.M.C.

Barry White, famous for his love songs in the 1970s and an active opponent of drugs and gangs, believes that Run-D.M.C.'s upbeat message can make for a better world. "The young people, blacks, white, Hispanic, all colors, love Run-D.M.C.," Barry says. "They have reached the nerve of the people through their . . . rapping genius."

All over the United States and Canada—and even in Europe—kids are dressing similarly to their straight-talking idols. The Run-D.M.C. style includes brimmed, felt hats, open sneakers, warm-up suits and long, black jackets. But group members claim that they have always sported the "b-boy look." "I never wore laces in my sneakers," says Jay "Jam Master Jay" Mizell. "It took too long to put them in."

Their story began on the tree-shaded streets of Hollis,

a neighborhood in Queens, New York. Residents proudly tell you that basketball legend Kareem Abdul-Jabbar grew up there. All three rappers—Mizell, Darryl "D.M.C." McDaniels, and Joseph "Run" Simmons—came from caring families which stressed education. But a few blocks away from their well-kept homes was a tougher neighborhood, plagued with drugs. Today, when members of the group tell fans "don't take drugs," they are speaking from experience. Saying no to drugs put Run-D.M.C. on the path to superstardom!

Although quiet, D.M.C. had a reputation in Hollis of being a creative young man. He wrote and illustrated his own comic books in his room and made up punchy rhymes which had his friends shaking their heads and roaring with laughter. When rap fever spread over to Hollis from the nearby Bronx, he teamed up with Jay. Jay was already known in the neighborhood as a sensational disc jockey. According to Run, "In Hollis, Jay was like Fonzie. He was the best DJ, the man everyone in Hollis knew."

Meanwhile, Run's older brother, Russell, was making such a mark as a manager of music acts that the movie *Krush Groove* was later based on his career. He was renting out ballrooms, hiring disc jockeys and charging party-goers seven dollars apiece to dance to the music he offered. Sometimes, Russell let twelve-year-old Run grab the microphone and rap to the dancers: "DJ Run, son of a gun/Always plays music and has big fun."

D.M.C. (left) and Run (right) rap in a concert with a little help from Jam Master Jay (in back).

By the end of high school, the three Run-D.M.C. members were hosting parties together. Russell Simmons had founded a management company handling rap acts like Kurtis Blow, and he was willing to help the group secure a record contract. Their single, "It's Like That," was released in March, 1983, and received airplay on black radio stations nationally.

D.M.C. holds up *King of Rock* and makes a little joke for the camera, but Jay doesn't seem too amused—he's probably seen it before.

Yet the boys were not sure if rap would be a reliable career, so they enrolled in college. D.M.C. majored in business at St. John's University. Run took general courses at LaGuardia Community College. Jay studied mortuary science at Queens College. "Everyone said rap was a fad," he recalls. "I knew death wasn't a fad, so I majored in mortuary science."

The group's second single, "Hard Times," soared to number eleven on *Billboard* magazine's black music chart. "I thought, 'We're set,'" D.M.C. says. "I knew that nothing could stop us now. We all took a leave of absence from school that turned out to be permanent."

All of the group members still live in Hollis, where Run is raising a family. "I'm a real family man now," he brags. "I even took them (wife Valerie and daughter Vanessa, born in 1983) to Europe...and we had a ball. I'm the kind of guy who gets lonely after a show and takes a flight home."

The bright lights of success and happiness have not blinded the group to the problems facing American teenagers. "I don't have a big mansion and beautiful clothes," Run says. "I see the crack on the corner. I need to get rid of this thing."

The Beastie Boys and L. L. Cool J (in red hat) with their producer
Rick Rubin (in beard)

Other Rappers

L.L. Cool J

Also from Hollis is young, showy James Todd Smith, known to most of the world as L.L. Cool J. The handsome entertainer is hardly acclaimed for his modesty — the "L.L." in his stage name stands for "Ladies Love," as in "ladies love Cool J."

L.L. was raised in his grandparents' two-story house. His parents were separated and his grandparents helped his mother raise him. They encouraged him to participate in wholesome activities. Says his grandmother, Ellen Griffith, "He sang in the church choir, he studied karate, he played football and Little League baseball, he got good grades in school. We tried to keep him occupied. We didn't want him to become a street kid."

His late grandfather, Eugene Griffith, served as a musical role model for the boy. The elder Griffith played tenor saxophone and guitar.

At age ten, L.L. heard his first rap record. He immediately knew his calling. The Griffiths considered music a more productive undertaking than neighborhood bicycle racing and bought their grandson $2,000 worth of recording equipment. It was money well spent. By the time he was thirteen years old, L.L. was sending homemade cassette tapes to record companies.

One tape ended up in the hands of Rick Rubin, the "boy genius" producer of rap records. Rubin and Russell Simmons produced L.L.'s first single, "I Need a Beat," in 1984. It sold over 100,000 copies and L.L.'s career was launched.

An appearance in the *Krush Groove* movie gained L.L. major publicity. The fans he made through his singles and his movie appearance were waiting for his first album, *Radio*, and quickly bought 600,000 copies after it was released.

His next record, *Bigger and Deffer*, rose to number four on the pop chart. He claims followers' adoration is based on his style. "My grandmother told me I should be a lawyer because I talk so much. Now, that's my job—I talk. And talk is not cheap, when you talk the right way."

Some record company executives have suggested that L.L. move to Hollywood, but the rapper is staying in Hollis. He says, "I don't want to lose touch with real life and real people, like my grandmother."

Whodini

In the early part of this century, magician Harry Houdini astonished audiences by escaping from sealed bank safes and other confinements. The rap group, Whodini, have more in common with the magician than a like-sounding name. Members Jalil Hutchins, John "Ecstasy" Fletcher, and Drew "Grandmaster Dee" Carter long ago escaped the confines of black radio. They have won over listeners who value rap put to quality music. They're like the magician in another way as well: Whodini always keeps fans guessing. Their likeable style keeps changing and developing.

From the beginning, the group always aimed for the smoothest sound possible. Their first single, "Magic's Wand," was co-produced by English studio king Thomas Dolby, a man renowned for perfection in setting music patterns. Since then, Whodini has released three big-selling albums, *Whodini*, *Escape*, and *Back in Black*. Their attention to sound as well as words has produced material in which the music and melody appeal as well as the lyrics and the beat.

Among Whodini's boosters is the *People* magazine reviewer who wrote about the rappers' "silky and attractive voices."

The group puts just as much care into their concerts as they do into their records. Back when the world was learning about hip-hop, Whodini was the first bunch of rappers to perform with break dancers.

Listeners are told to use personal setbacks as growing experiences. On *Back in Black*, Whodini sings, "Sometimes you got to be down and out/Before you can find out what it's all about/I guess really to understand the story/You got to feel the pain as well as the glory."

So impressive is Whodini's message that a New York museum has ensured that they will be studied by future generations. The group's "Big Mouth" video is in the Museum of Modern Art's permanent collection.

Kurtis Blow

Kurtis Blow's sixth album, *Kingdom Blow*, declares him the "king of rap." In some ways, the boast is true.

Kurtis has been a rapper almost since the beginning. In his Harlem neighborhood he was the class clown, a popular guy. He wrote poetry when he was a kid. A short time after first hearing rap music, Curtis Walker had adopted the stage name Kurtis Blow and was emceeing at clubs near his home. So confident was he in his rapping skills that he frequently let others come up to

31

the mike to rhyme to the audience. One youngster, Joseph "Run" Simmons, even called himself "son of Kurtis Blow."

In 1979, Blow became the first rapper to be signed to a major recording label, Mercury/Polygram Records. He was also the first rapper to have a song go gold (sell 500,000 copies). His gold-selling "Christmas Rappin'" and its follow-up, "The Breaks," helped spark a global "rap attack." Suddenly, rap was being played on radio stations all over, and rap music was selling not only in rural America but Europe as well.

At the same time as he has guided his own career, Blow has contributed to the songs of other top rappers. He has produced groups such as The Fat Boys, Run-D.M.C., Lovebug Starski, Sweet Gee, and Dr. Jekyll and Mr. Hyde.

The *New York Daily News* wrote that his performance in *Krush Groove* was "especially note-worthy... a dynamic presence." He has also appeared in the films *Cry of the City* and *Bamboo Cross*.

Companies like Lee Jeans and Sprite have chosen him to endorse their products because of his healthy image. His fans know about his crusade against drinking and drugs. He urges blacks to study their heritage, and he has been involved in projects honoring slain civil rights leader Dr. Martin Luther King, Jr. His 1985 song "America" reviewed American history and promoted brotherhood.

There are many more messages inside Kurtis Blow. "I'm a poet and I know it and I like to show it," he raps.

The Fat Boys

There's no law stating that all music should be serious. "Good thing," say Darren "The Human Beat Box" Robinson, Damon "Kool Rock Ski" Wimbley, and Mark "Prince Markie Dee" Morales. As The Fat Boys, the trio has made audiences move their feet in dance and hold their stomachs in laughter.

Originally called the Disco 3, the New Yorkers first came into the public spotlight when they placed second in a 1983 rap contest sponsored by Coca-Cola. They accepted a $5,000 stereo system and almost went home without realizing that there was another prize—a contract with Sutra Records.

The Fat Boys: almost half a ton of fun

After releasing their single "Reality," Disco 3 embarked on a tour of Europe. An incident on the tour led to the change in the group's name. In Switzerland, their manager, Charles Stettler, noticed that the rappers' hotel bill showed an additional $350 charge—for food. Rather than scold them, Stettler renamed the combo The Fat Boys and encouraged them to sing about their large waists and love of eating.

The gimmick worked. The Fat Boys are the clown princes of rap. They have penned tunes about sitting down at the kitchen table and about holding up a fast food store. Their first two albums, *The Fat Boys*, and *The Fat Boys Are Back*, went gold. Their third, *Big and Beautiful*, took off in sales as well. Many insist that the group's natural humor saved some scenes in *Krush Groove*. They were so appealing in that movie that they landed a deal with Warner Brothers to do three more movies. Their first, *Disorderlies*, about three zany hospital workers, reminded many viewers of the madcap Three Stooges and Marx Brothers films. They have appeared on a commercial for SWATCH Watches and are marketing their own line of jeans. They've even made extra-large football star William "The Refrigerator" Perry an "honorary Fat Boy."

The Fat Boys have proven that fat not only is funny— it's also profitable.

UTFO

Eric B. and Rakim

Public Enemy

The Future of Rap

Rap is still a new music form. It is expanding every day, and the sound has grown wide enough to include scores of future stars. Some rap is rock-based, some is funk, and some is very close to the original "street" sound.

A few of the present stars will definitely have a noticeable impact on the music. Doug E. Fresh, singer of "All the Way to Heaven" and "The Show," is fast becoming a radio hero. White rappers the Beastie Boys created "the party record of the year," New York's *Village Voice* said, with their 1986 album *Licensed to Ill*. Their subversive humor has made them thousands of young fans. Melle Mel's song "Vice" helped the soundtrack from the "Miami Vice" television show sell 1.3 million copies in two weeks.

Run-D.M.C., in the meantime, is putting out their own line of "B-boy" clothes. They made another movie in 1986, a mystery-adventure. The group members describe *Tougher Than Leather* as "a cross between *48 Hrs.* and *Rambo*." Of course, Run, D.M.C., and Jay are the film's heroes. The bad guys are drug dealers.

Jam Master Jay, Run, and D.M.C. set up a shot in *Tougher Than Leather.* With them are Rick Rubin, their record producer and the movie's director and co-executive producer, and Feliks Parnell, the director of photography.

Of course, there are still plenty who are afraid of rap and won't listen to its message. The image of the music was not helped by the violence which broke out at several concerts in 1986. Those who dislike the music were ready to cry, "Rap causes violence!" Police observers, however, point out that violence occurs whenever rival gang members go to the same concert. The kids in the inner city who join gangs often like rap's gritty street sound. As one cop put it after fighting cancelled a Run-D.M.C. show at the Long Beach Arena, "Run-D.M.C. gets a bad rap because of the crowds they draw. There are long-held grudges between these gangs, and when they converge in one place, the paybacks will come . . . even if Reagan was speaking, there'd have been bloodshed." Run-D.M.C. went back to the Los Angeles area after the Long Beach concert and appeared on a daylong radio show urging an end to gang violence.

Rap's positive messages greatly outweigh the problems caused by a few of its fans. And its messages seem to be spreading.

The time is near when all of America will be bopping to rap. Writing in the *New York Times*, Robert Palmer observed, "The music seems well on its way to crossing over from black to white teenagers much as rhythm and blues did when it became rock-and-roll in the '50s." It remains to be seen if rap will be just as revolutionary.

The Beastie Boys: King Ad-Rock, Mike D, MCA

Photo credits:

Adrian Boot/Retna Ltd., p. 2
George DuBose/London Features International, p. 6
Chase Roe/Retna Ltd., pp. 10, 16, 18, 20, 22, 24, 36 (center)
Andy Catlin/Retna Ltd., p. 13
Cyndi Palmano/Retna Ltd., p. 26
Rush Productions, p. 29
PolyGram Records, p. 31
Phototeque, p. 33
Tin Pan Apple, p. 34
Waring Abbott/Rush Productions, p. 36 (top)
Lloyd Nelson/Rush Productions, p. 36 (bottom)
Sebastian Piras/Howard Bloom Organization Ltd., p. 38
Sunny Bak/Rush Productions, p. 40

Front cover photograph by George DuBose/London Features International